A DAY IN THE LIFE OF A
Construction Foreman

Text and photographs by Gayle Jann

Troll Associates

Library of Congress Cataloging in Publication Data

Jann, Gayle.
   A day in the life of a construction foreman.

   Summary: Follows a construction foreman on the site of
a skyscraper through his day as he meets with engineers to
discuss the building's electrical systems, consults with
the safety officer and layout man, and checks the voltage
in a temporary light room.
   1. Spaulding, Brian—Juvenile literature. 2. Building
—United States—Superintendence—Biography—Juvenile
literature. 3. Building—Superintendence—Vocational
guidance—Juvenile literature. 4. Electricians—
Vocational guidance—Juvenile literature. [1. Building—
Superintendence. 2. Spaulding, Brian. 3. Building.
4. Occupations] I. Title.
TH140.S58J36   1988   690'.092'4   87-13761
ISBN 0-8167-1121-6 (lib. bdg.)
ISBN 0-8167-1122-4 (pbk.)

Special thanks to L. K. Comstock & Co., Inc. and Tishman Construction of
New York for their assistance and cooperation.

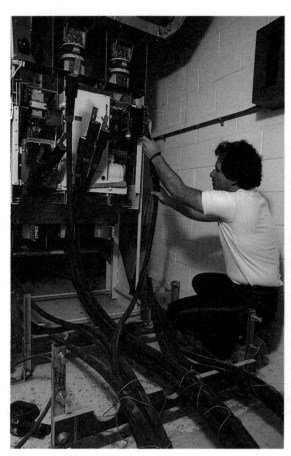
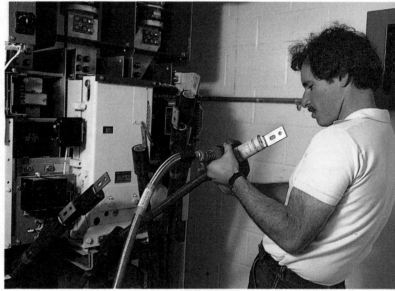

Brian Spaulding is an electrician who is a construction foreman on the site of a skyscraper. He is one of many foremen in charge of the various construction crews. His day sometimes begins in one of the building's "network protector rooms." These are special areas that control the electricity coming into the building.

Brian drills into the concrete floor to install a bracket that will help support the transformer cables. Another electrician inspects the cables on the floor below, where the transformers are located. The transformers change high voltage electricity into low voltage power that is fed through the cables to the network protector rooms above.

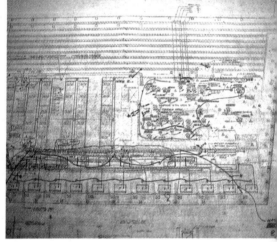

Brian meets with one of the site engineers to go over the plans for the building's electrical system. When electricity passes through the network protectors, it is sent to every part of the building. Lighting systems, elevators, fire alarms, intercoms, and air conditioning systems will all need a constant supply of electricity.

Brian gets together with the foremen who supervise the carpenters and high-iron workers. They must go over the plans for the work they will be doing. Many crews work together to build a skyscraper, and all the foremen must work as a team. Like other construction workers, Brian wears a hard hat when he is outdoors on the site.

The safety officer for the site talks briefly with Brian as he makes his inspections. The safety officer meets with the foremen on a regular basis. Part of each foreman's job is making sure that safety standards are observed on the site. Each foreman is responsible not only for the work done by members of his crew, but also for their safety.

High above the city, Brian consults with the "lay-out man." Together they go over the plans for one of the floors. The layout man measures and marks the positions for trenches in the flooring. The trenches will house three trays—one for telephone wires, one for electric wires, and one for wires that will be used by computer systems.

Brian assists an apprentice who is installing covers on wiring trenches. When the trenches are in place and complete, concrete will be poured to the edge. When the concrete has dried, the covers on the trenches will be lifted and the wiring for each room will be put in.

Where the wires go from floor to floor, they must travel through special pipes, or "conduits." An apprentice uses a torch to cut holes in the flooring for the pipes. All of the building trades have apprenticeship programs, so that younger people can learn on the job. Apprentices are supervised by senior members of their crews.

When holes have been cut in the floor for pipes to pass through, the floor must be strengthened. At ground level, a metal worker cuts steel bars that will be used to reinforce some of the flooring beams. Metal workers wear special goggles to protect their eyes from the bright light as their hot torches cut through the metal.

Once the wiring trenches are installed and the floor has been reinforced, the concrete can be poured. Special trucks deliver the concrete. Cement, sand, gravel and water are mixed in a revolving drum on the truck, then poured through a spout and down a chute. This concrete mixture is quickly taken to each floor where it is needed.

The concrete is spread with a rake. Then workers slide a long wooden bar back and forth to level the surface. This process is called "striking off." Then a hand-held wooden "float" is used to smooth the surface. Wherever the concrete will not be covered over later, the final smoothing, or "floating," is done with a metal float.

After lunch, Brian talks with the foreman of the sheet metal workers. The sheet metal workers build and install a complex network of metal ducts. The ducts will carry ventilation, heating, and air conditioning throughout the building. Large sections are connected by tightening a metal band around the duct where the pieces join.

The sheet metal from which the ducts are made is "galvanized," or coated with rust-resistant zinc, to protect against corrosion. After the last pieces of ductwork are bolted together, all the ducts are wrapped in insulation. This will help prevent condensation when the air conditioning is turned on. It also helps keep operating costs at a minimum.

Today is an important day on the site. The "topping iron"—the last piece of the structural framework—will be put into place by the high-iron workers. This is a cause for celebration, and Brian wants to watch. The topping iron is painted white, and has been signed by all the contractors. It is decorated with flags for the ceremony.

After the ceremony, Brian rides the temporary elevator down to the ground floor, to meet with the foreman of the ornamental iron workers. The temporary elevator is used for construction equipment and crews, so it is on the outside of the structure, where it can be easily loaded with supplies as they are delivered to the site.

The ornamental iron workers need electricity as they work on the building's decorative columns. These polished stainless steel columns will be installed both outside and inside the building. Steel mounting brackets are attached to the unpolished side. The brackets will anchor the columns to the frame of the building.

Great care must be taken so that the mirror-like surface of the stainless steel columns will not be scratched. The heavy columns are carefully lifted with a "block and tackle"—a chain and pulley arrangement. Once in place, the columns are riveted into position.

The building's exterior will be made of polished imperial red granite. Workers called "stone erectors" attach blocks of the granite to a huge crane that will lift the blocks up the side of the building. Each piece of granite is marked to show on what floor it will be installed, as well as on which side of the building—north, south, east or west.

The building is 47 stories high, so the stone erectors must communicate by walkie-talkie with the hoisting operator, who is working the crane. The men on the upper floors guide the granite blocks into place. Then they bolt and weld the blocks to the steel frame of the building.

As the building is closed in, the interior grows so dark that temporary lights must be used in many areas. Brian checks the wiring on a "streamer," one of the temporary lights used by the construction crews. Streamers are used until the permanent electrical systems have been installed. This may take as long as 18 months.

Brian checks the voltage in the temporary power system. All of the electricity used on the site comes from this system, which is separate from the permanent power system. Electrical crews install the permanent power system floor by floor as the building rises, but for safety reasons it is not turned on until the system is completed.

The wiring for the permanent power system will run through electrical pipes of all sizes. Brian uses both large and small pipe-bending machines to create smooth curves, with no sharp angles. This is important because the wires must be "snaked" through *after* the pipes are installed. Sharp angles would make it very difficult to push the wires through.

While Brian works with lightweight electrical pipe, plumbers install heavy cast-iron waste pipe that will be concealed above the ceiling. Each section of the pipe weighs about 100 pounds, so a plumber's apprentice is needed to help with the job. Another plumber uses a "torque wrench" to tighten the bands connecting the sections of pipe.

Brian takes the temporary elevator down to ground level to meet with some of the carpenters. On a skyscraper site, carpenters frequently work with galvanized steel, because it is strong and fireproof, and will not corrode. The steel used for doorway supports must be carefully measured. The frame must be level and square.

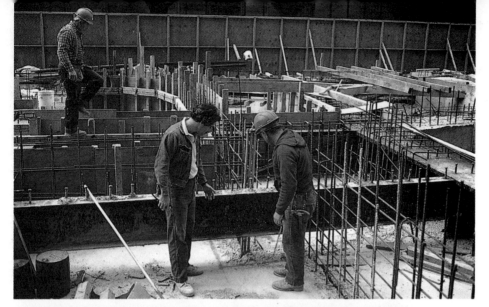

Brian checks on the progress of a crew of carpenters building wooden forms for ornamental concrete planters. The forms will support the concrete until it hardens. Metal rods will give added strength to the concrete. Later, crews of electricians will install the wiring for a special lighting system around the planters.

Brian likes to keep up with the progress of the other crews by visiting their work sites from time to time. A bricklayer works on a decorative masonry wall inside the building. The laying of bricks may look simple, but it takes skill to be able to work quickly, while the "mortar" is wet. Each brick must be level and properly set.

Brian stops to talk with a steamfitter before checking on the building's fire alarm system. The steamfitters install the pipes for the heating and sprinkler systems. When the sprinkler system is finished, its pipes will be filled with water under pressure. If a fire should occur, the heat would set off the sprinklers, automatically releasing the water.

Each of the steel beams and columns in the building's framework must be coated with fireproofing material. Huge sheets of plastic "mask off" the area as the fireproofing is sprayed. This is done on each floor as the building rises. Later, welders must scrape away the fireproofing before they can weld mounting brackets to the beams or columns.

Sprinklers and fireproofing help keep a building safe. The fire alarm system, however, is one of the most important safety systems in the building. The entire alarm system will be monitored around the clock once the building is occupied. Brian consults with another electrician, who is making final wiring connections in the fire alarm panel.

As Brian leaves the construction site at the end of the day, the tower of the skyscraper is silhouetted against the evening sky. Building a skyscraper requires many crews of specialized workers with one common goal. Brian enjoys his work and is proud to be a construction foreman—a member of the team that changes the city's skyline.